Pride and Prejudice

Lightbox Literature Studies

Piper Whelan

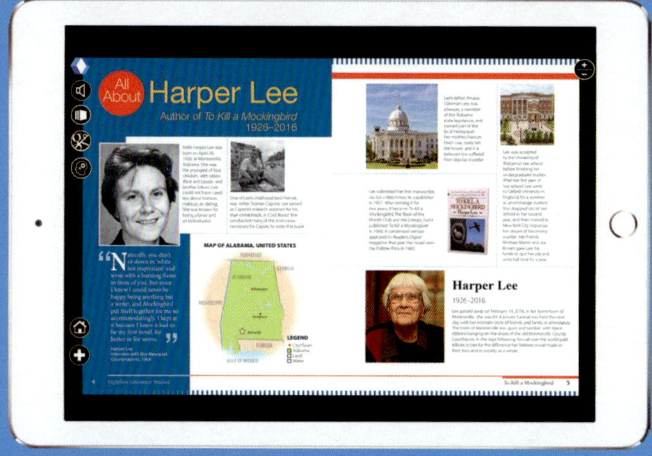

Lightbox is an all-inclusive digital solution for the teaching and learning of curriculum topics in an original, groundbreaking way. Lightbox is based on National Curriculum Standards.

STANDARD FEATURES OF LIGHTBOX

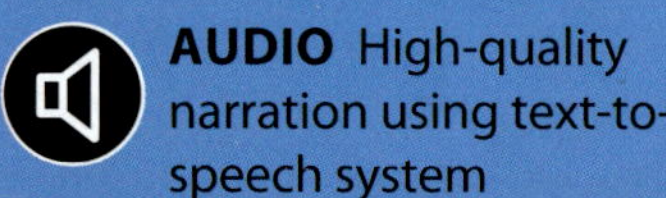
AUDIO High-quality narration using text-to-speech system

VIDEOS Embedded high-definition video clips

ACTIVITIES Printable PDFs that can be emailed and graded

WEBLINKS Curated links to external, child-safe resources

SLIDESHOWS Pictorial overviews of key concepts

TRANSPARENCIES Step-by-step layering of maps, diagrams, charts, and timelines

INTERACTIVE MAPS Interactive maps and aerial satellite imagery

QUIZZES Ten multiple choice questions that are automatically graded and emailed for teacher assessment

KEY WORDS Matching key concepts to their definitions

MORE Extra information and details on the subject

FIRST HAND Letters, diaries, and other primary sources

DOCS Speeches, newspaper articles, and other historical documents

Contents

PRIDE AND PREJUDICE
JANE AUSTEN
EDITED BY DONALD GRAY
A NORTON CRITICAL EDITION
THIRD EDITION

EXTENSION ACTIVITY

Analyzing a Painting

Students will complete an analysis of a painting or portrait. An exemplary analysis will meet the following criteria.

- Identifies the artist and the date on which the painting was created
- Describes the subject of the painting
- Places the painting in a historical context
- Describes the imagery and subjects illustrated by the painting
- Explains any symbolism found in the painting
- Determines any messages or meanings the artist may be trying to convey
- Explains feelings or moods evoked by the painting
- Presents information in a clear, concise manner
- Uses correct spelling, grammar, and punctuation

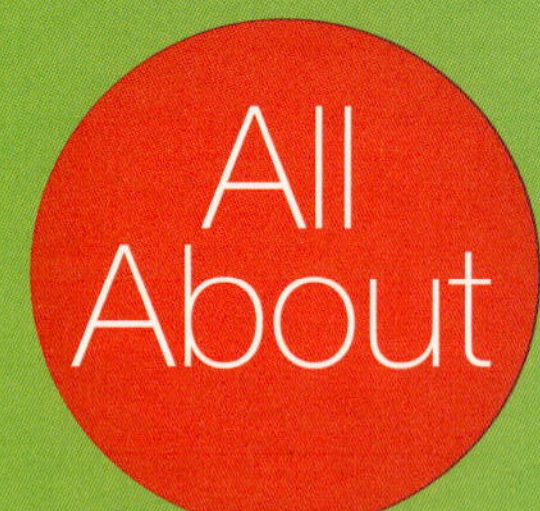

Jane Austen

Author of *Pride and Prejudice* 1775–1817

Jane Austen was born on December 16, 1775, in Steventon, Hampshire, United Kingdom. She was the seventh child in her family. Her father, Reverend George Austen, was the rector of their village. Her mother, Cassandra Leigh Austen, was known for her wit and humor. Austen's family was known to be affectionate, and together they enjoyed creative pursuits, such as writing and acting in plays. The children were encouraged to learn as much as possible and had access to their father's library. Austen's only sister, Cassandra, was her best friend. They were sent to boarding school together during their adolescent years. At school, they both caught **typhus**, and then came home when their family was unable to afford their tuition.

> "Know your own happiness. Want for nothing but patience—or give it a more fascinating name: Call it hope."
>
> Jane Austen
> *Sense and Sensibility*, 1811

MAP OF THE UNITED KINGDOM

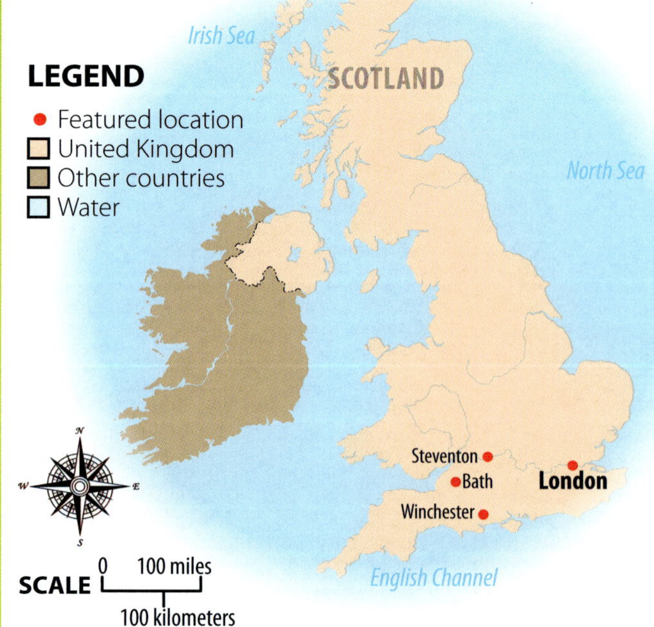

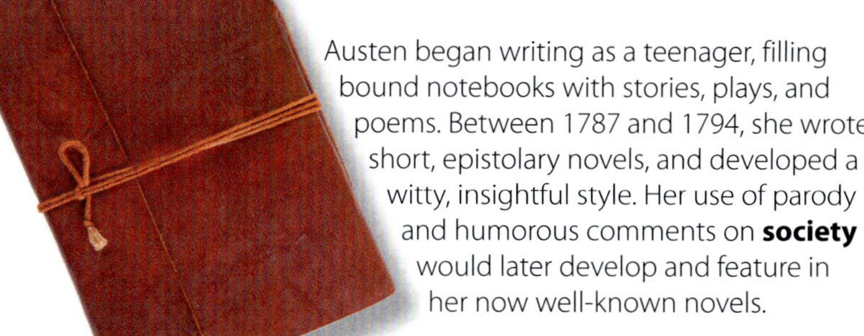

Austen began writing as a teenager, filling bound notebooks with stories, plays, and poems. Between 1787 and 1794, she wrote short, epistolary novels, and developed a witty, insightful style. Her use of parody and humorous comments on **society** would later develop and feature in her now well-known novels.

As an adult, Austen lived with her parents and sister, and had a busy social and home life. In addition to writing, she is said to have enjoyed playing the piano and dancing. Austen never married, but is speculated to have had a few romantic connections. In 1801, she moved to Bath with her family, but they found themselves dealing with financial instability after her father died in 1805. She moved continually with her mother and sister until 1809, when her brother Edward provided them with a cottage home on his estate at Chawton.

Austen wrote the first version of the story that became *Pride and Prejudice* between October 1796 and August 1797. Originally titled *First Impressions*, the novel was rejected when her father sent it to a London publisher. It was not until she was in her 30s that Austen began to anonymously publish her novels, starting with *Sense and Sensibility* in 1811. *Pride and Prejudice* was released in January 1813 and became a hit with readers. She later published two more novels, *Emma* and *Mansfield Park*.

In 1816, Austen became ill with what experts now believe was Addison's disease. She continued to work hard on new novels, but her illness weakened her to a point where she was forced to stop writing. Austen died on July 18, 1817, in Winchester, Hampshire, at the age of 41. After her death, Austen's brother Henry helped publish two of her last works, *Persuasion* and *Northanger Abbey*, in her own name.

TEACHER NOTES

Google Maps

Jane Austen's House Museum, Winchester-Road, Chawton, Alton, United Kingdom

Use street view to explore the cottage in Chawton where Jane Austen lived for the last eight years of her life, now a museum with an exhibit dedicated to the author.

Weblink

Pretty Words, Jane; Would that You Were Too

Analyze the *New York Times* article about the appearance of Jane Austen.

1. Why is it important for Austen's readers to discover her appearance? Why has her image been manipulated in recent publications?
2. How did her appearance influence Austen's life in the eighteenth century? What effects did her appearance have on her writing career? How might Austen's appearance affect her life and writing career if she lived in our contemporary era?

EXTENSION ACTIVITY

Researching for a Writing Assignment

Students will complete a thorough research process to prepare for a writing assignment, and organize their research in a logical manner that supports their writing. An exemplary research process will meet the following criteria.

- Creates a goal for the research, based on the topic and working thesis
- Creates specific, thoughtful, and inventive research questions that are relevant to the topic of the writing assignment
- Produces a list of categories, key words, and related ideas to effectively assist in researching
- Uses high-quality sources that pertain to the topic and come in a variety of formats, such as books, journals, primary sources, websites, and databases
- Determines accuracy of all sources
- Uses sources that provide balanced research and various perspectives on the topic in question
- Takes notes to highlight the key facts and ideas in order to answer all research questions
- Extracts relevant, detailed information from the sources during the note-taking process
- Organizes the research notes in a clear and concise manner
- Organizes the research notes logically and in a way that sets up the information and ideas for analysis and the writing process
- Analyzes the information and produces ideas and points to support the working thesis
- Uses an effective and suitable format to present all research
- Properly cites all sources used

Setting of the Novel

Pride and Prejudice is primarily set in the rural English village of Longbourn. The Bennet family's home in Longbourn reflects rural village life for those who were well-to-do at the time, and the novel also provides a look at the lives of the upper **classes** through scenes set at Mr. Darcy's estate. Elizabeth Bennet and her sisters also visit other estates, such as Netherfield, and towns such as nearby Meryton.

The Bennet House

"They were not the only objects of Mr. Collins's admiration. The hall, the dining-room, and all its furniture, were examined and praised; and his commendation of every thing would have touched Mrs. Bennet's heart, but for the mortifying supposition of his viewing it all as his own future property. The dinner too, in its turn, was highly admired; and he begged to know to which of his fair cousins the excellence of its cookery was owing. But here he was set right by Mrs. Bennet, who assured him with some asperity that they were very well able to keep a good cook, and that her daughters had nothing to do in the kitchen."

Chapter 13

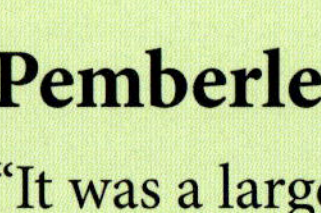

Pemberley

"It was a large, well-proportioned room, handsomely fitted up. Elizabeth, after slightly surveying it, went to a window to enjoy its prospect. The hill, crowned with wood, from which they had descended, receiving increased abruptness from the distance, was a beautiful object. Every disposition of the ground was good; and she looked on the whole scene—the river, the trees scattered on its banks, and the winding of the valley, as far as she could trace it—with delight. As they passed into other rooms, these objects were taking different positions; but from every window there were beauties to be seen. The rooms were lofty and handsome, and their furniture suitable to the fortune of their proprietor; but Elizabeth saw, with admiration of his taste, that it was neither gaudy nor uselessly fine; with less of splendour, and more real elegance, than the furniture of Rosings."

Chapter 43

During this time period, the class known as the **gentry** exerted influence on society. Accordingly, *Pride and Prejudice* operates within this world, and focuses on issues related to class, property, and money, illustrating the social landscape of the time. The gentry was a wide-ranging class, comprised of both wealthy landowners and the professional classes. While Mr. Bennet is considered a country gentleman who lives a comfortable life, does not have to work, and can afford to employ servants, Mr. Darcy is a member of the landed gentry, who inherited his home and land.

The 1995 BBC television adaptation of *Pride and Prejudice* saw Lyme Park stand in as Pemberley Hall, Mr. Darcy's estate. This estate in Cheshire, which is a county in England's Peak District, was constructed from the sixteenth through the nineteenth centuries, and was home to aristocratic families. This grand estate reflects the lifestyle of the nobility in Britain during this era.

TEACHER NOTES

 Video

LYME -'LYMESCAPES' - by Dave Thompson

Explore Lyme Park, and compare the lifestyles of aristocracy and gentry at the end of the eighteenth century.

1. Why do you think Lyme Park was chosen as the set for Mr. Darcy's Pemberley Hall? How do the building and its gardens reflect the lifestyle of the English aristocracy of the eighteenth century? Justify your answers.
2. What was the importance of country estates for aristocratic families? How did their lifestyles differ from those of the professional classes? Give specific examples.

Weblink

The Historical Context of *Pride and Prejudice*

Evaluate the historical context of the late eighteenth and early nineteenth centuries, and the role it played in Austen's novel.

1. Why was ownership of land the key to economic prosperity during this historical period? What does the expression, "the taint of trade" mean? Why were the laborer classes "tainted"?
2. What was the role of women in the society of the Georgian Era? How did this role differ from the one assumed by women in other historical periods? Why?

EXTENSION ACTIVITY

Analyzing Famous Speeches as Arguments

Students will analyze a well-known speech as an argument and write a response. An exemplary analysis will meet the following criteria.

- Presents a strong thesis that is based on analysis of the argument presented in the speech and how the argument is presented
- Consistently uses strong textual evidence to support the thesis
- Presents an engaging and effective introduction, body, and conclusion
- Structures the analysis in a logical order
- Develops a thorough analysis of the speech
- Uses clear prose to present the student's voice and perspective
- Identifies the main points presented in the speech
- Identifies the speaker and infers how his or her life may have shaped this argument
- Identifies when and where the speech was given
- Determines the speech's intended audience
- Analyzes how the speaker makes his or her argument
- Uses strong evidence from the speech to show how the speaker supports his or her argument
- Analyzes the language used to convey the speech's argument
- Demonstrates understanding of the historical and societal context in which the speech was given and connects that context to the speaker's argument
- Properly integrates quotations
- Properly cites all sources used

Time Period of the Novel

Pride and Prejudice is set sometime during the Napoleonic Wars, which took place during the late eighteenth and early nineteenth centuries. During this time, Britain's participation in the war shaped life at home in many ways. This time period also coincided with what is known as the Regency period. Austen's novels hint at the events going on in the world at this time, but are also concerned with the status of women in this era, especially regarding **inheritance**.

Snapshot

The **Napoleonic Wars** lasted **23 years**.

During the Napoleonic Wars, it is estimated that about a **quarter of a million men** served in the **British army**.

Almost **everyone** in the **British middle classes could read by 1800**, which is when literacy rates for all of Britain began to increase.

The Napoleonic Wars

"When is your turn to come? You will hardly bear to be long outdone by Jane. Now is your time. Here are officers enough at Meryton to disappoint all the young ladies in the country. Let Wickham be your man."

Mr. Bennet, Chapter 24

A Daughter's Inheritance

"Mr. Bennet's property consisted almost entirely in an estate of two thousand a year, which, unfortunately for his daughters, was entailed, in default of heirs male, on a distant relation; and their mother's fortune, though ample for her situation in life, could but ill supply the deficiency of his. Her father had been an attorney in Meryton, and had left her four thousand pounds."

Chapter 7

Britain was in conflict with France for a number of years around the start of the nineteenth century, during the time when Austen wrote her novels. Napoleon Bonaparte, the emperor of post-Revolutionary France, waged wars in an effort to expand France's empire. In addition to the regular army, a **militia** was raised on England's southeast coast in the event of a French invasion. Napoleon was defeated in 1815 by Britain and other European nations at the Battle of Waterloo in Belgium. In *Pride and Prejudice*, militia officers such as Mr. Wickham illustrate the presence of the military in everyday life, in the event of an invasion by Napoleon's forces.

The Regency, taking place from 1811 to 1820, was the era in which Britain's Prince of Wales, who became known as the Prince Regent, ruled in the place of his father, King George III. George III was deemed unable to rule after he began to show symptoms of what is now thought to be a disorder called porphyria. This illness, which affects hemoglobin production, caused the king to behave unpredictably. Although the Prince Regent was known for his extravagant indulgences, the Regency was a time that stressed the importance of **civility** and what was known as "**moral** seriousness."

Part of Mrs. Bennet's anxiety for her daughters to get married is due to the fact that her husband's estate is tied up, so her daughters would not be provided for if they were single after he died. Marriage offered security at a time when inheritance laws did not always benefit women. The inheritance law affecting Mr. Bennet's estate, called an entail, was created to keep large estates intact by passing property to one male heir, rather than dividing it between a number of heirs. The Bennet home and estate would go to an extended family member, Mr. Collins, instead of being shared among the five daughters. Marriage, then, could provide financial security for a woman who was not legally permitted to inherit land or money from her father.

TEACHER NOTES

Document

Draft of a Message of Abdication from George III to the Parliament

Analyze the text of the 1783 speech with which King George III planned to announce his abdication.

1. George III planned to abdicate during a political crisis, but the abdication was not finalized. In your opinion, why did the king, who was ready to abdicate the throne during a political crisis, never plan to abdicate when he developed his mental health condition? Formulate some hypotheses and give evidence to back up your position.
2. Why was the reason for the political crisis, the loss of the North American colonies, never mentioned in King George's draft? What does the style of the text tell us about the perception that the king had of his own power?

Weblink

Courtship, love and marriage in Jane Austen's novels

Assess the importance of marriage in the Georgian era and compare it to our concept of marriage today.

1. Why was love a secondary aspect in marriages during the Georgian era? What was the social role of marriage at that time? Why?
2. How did the concept of marriage change over time? Do you think that marriage would have the same function in Austen's novels if they were written today? Why or why not? Explain your answer.

EXTENSION ACTIVITY

Writing a Short Story

Students will choose an excerpt from the novel and use it as their inspiration in writing a short story. An exemplary short story will meet the following criteria.

- Engages the reader from the opening line
- Establishes a clear, consistent point of view
- Introduces a narrator and a setting
- Develops an engaging conflict at the heart of the narrative to build tension and keep the reader interested
- Develops characters and events through purposeful and well-crafted literary devices
- Creates a logical progression of events in the narrative that build upon each other using various techniques
- Explores ideas, concepts, and writing styles with creativity and originality
- Demonstrates a high level of skill in using appropriate narrative techniques to tell the story
- Concludes the narrative in a thoughtful, effective manner appropriate to the narrative
- Uses varied, purposeful diction and syntax to affect style and serve the narrative
- Writes with clarity, imagination, and a unique, personal voice
- Does not use stereotypes or clichés
- Uses effective, believable dialogue
- Uses correct spelling, grammar, and punctuation

Conflict in the Novel

In literature, conflict is a struggle between two or more opposing forces, creating tension that must be resolved. This is the main challenge that the protagonist faces throughout the story. This struggle is often between the protagonist and the antagonist, but there are other types of conflict found in literature. Conflict is a vital element in any piece of literature. Without it, there is no story.

The Four Major Types of Conflict in Literature

In man versus man, the protagonist struggles against an opposing character, usually the antagonist. This is a common type of conflict in fiction, and generally features the fight between good and evil. In *The Wizard of Oz*, Dorothy's quest to find a way home to Kansas is made difficult by the Wicked Witch of the West.

In man versus self, the protagonist fights an inner battle. The battle is often about a major decision. The internal issue then affects the character's actions and motivation. This type of conflict appears in *Lord of the Flies*, as a group of schoolboys who have been marooned on an island grapple with the instincts that lead them to violence.

In this type of conflict, the protagonist is opposed to the principles or actions of the community, or of society as a whole. This conflict is based upon the protagonist's beliefs or morals. In *The Grapes of Wrath*, the Joad family leaves the Oklahoma Dust Bowl in search of prosperity in California. They are unable to find work that supports them, and are thrown into a violent labor struggle.

In man versus nature, the protagonist faces an obstacle in nature. This many be an entire landscape or a symbolic representation of nature, such as an animal or natural disaster. This type of conflict is present in *The Road*, as an unnamed man and his son travel in a post-apocalyptic world, and try to survive in a desolate land.

Types of Conflict in *Pride and Prejudice*

The three main types of conflict in *Pride and Prejudice* are man versus self, man versus society, and man versus man. Each of these conflicts plays a major role in the story.

Man versus Self

"'How despicably have I acted?' she cried. – 'I, who have **prided** myself on my discernment! – I, who have **valued** myself on my abilities! who have often disdained the generous candour of my sister, and gratified my vanity, in useless or blameable distrust. – How humiliating is this discovery! – Yet, how just a humiliation! – Had I been in love, I could not have been more wretchedly blind. But vanity, not love, has been my folly...Till this moment, I never knew myself.'"

Elizabeth Bennet, Chapter 36

Elizabeth Bennet

Man versus Society

"But I tell you what, Miss Lizzy – if you take it into your head to go on refusing every offer of marriage in this way, you will never get a husband at all – and I am sure I do not know who is to maintain you when your father is dead. – I shall not be able to keep you – and so I warn you."

Mrs. Bennet, Chapter 20

Mrs. Bennet

Man versus Man

"My daughter and my nephew are formed for each other. They are descended, on the maternal side, from the same noble line; and, on the father's, from respectable, honourable, and ancient—though untitled—families. Their fortune on both sides is splendid. They are destined for each other by the voice of every member of their respective houses; and what is to divide them? The upstart pretensions of a young woman without family, connexions, or fortune. Is this to be endured! But it must not, shall not be!"

Lady Catherine de Bourgh, Chapter 56

Lady Catherine de Bourgh

TEACHER NOTES

More

The Types of Conflict in Pride and Prejudice

Analyze the excerpts from the novel revealing the types of conflict as they appear in *Pride and Prejudice.*

1. How do these excerpts of conflict reveal the novel's theme? How do they reveal character? Explain and defend your ideas.
2. Write an analysis of Austen's development of conflict between Elizabeth and Mr. Darcy. What deeper truths may be suggested about these characters as a result of their conflict?

Video

Pride and Prejudice: Mr. Darcy's First Appearance

Analyze how conflict is presented in this scene from the 1995 BBC adaptation of Austen's novel.

1. Why is the relationship between the two main characters presented as a conflict at the beginning of the novel? Is the novel's representation of the conflict matched in its adaptation? Why or why not?
2. Why is the conflict expressed without direct interaction between the two characters? Does this effectively convey the conflict between the characters? In which other ways could the conflict be portrayed? Justify your answers.

EXTENSION ACTIVITY

Analyzing a Letter

Students will assess a letter and write an analysis. An exemplary analysis will meet the following criteria.

- Identifies the topic of the letter
- Determines the date on which the letter was written
- Identifies the main points and opinions expressed by the author
- Determines any goals the letter's writer is trying to accomplish with his or her document
- Identifies the writer and recipient of the letter
- Presents background information about the writer and recipient
- Assesses the reliability of the letter's writer
- Analyzes any use of literary devices in the letter
- Differentiates between the facts and opinions stated by the writer
- Connects the letter to the societal and historical context in which it was written
- Infers additional information about the topic based on the content of the letter
- Uses a number of other resources to analyze the context in which the letter was written
- Uses correct spelling, grammar, and punctuation

Introducing the Characters

Writers use direct and indirect methods to reveal their characters. Successful writers tend to rely on indirect methods of character development. It is more effective to learn about characters by watching them in action rather than being told what they are like. When writers comment on their characters' personalities, they often do so through the eyes of other characters who see things from their own limited **perspectives**. Many of the character traits that are revealed in this way come from the perspective of Elizabeth Bennet, whose thoughts are provided for the reader in this third-person narration.

Major Characters in *Pride and Prejudice*

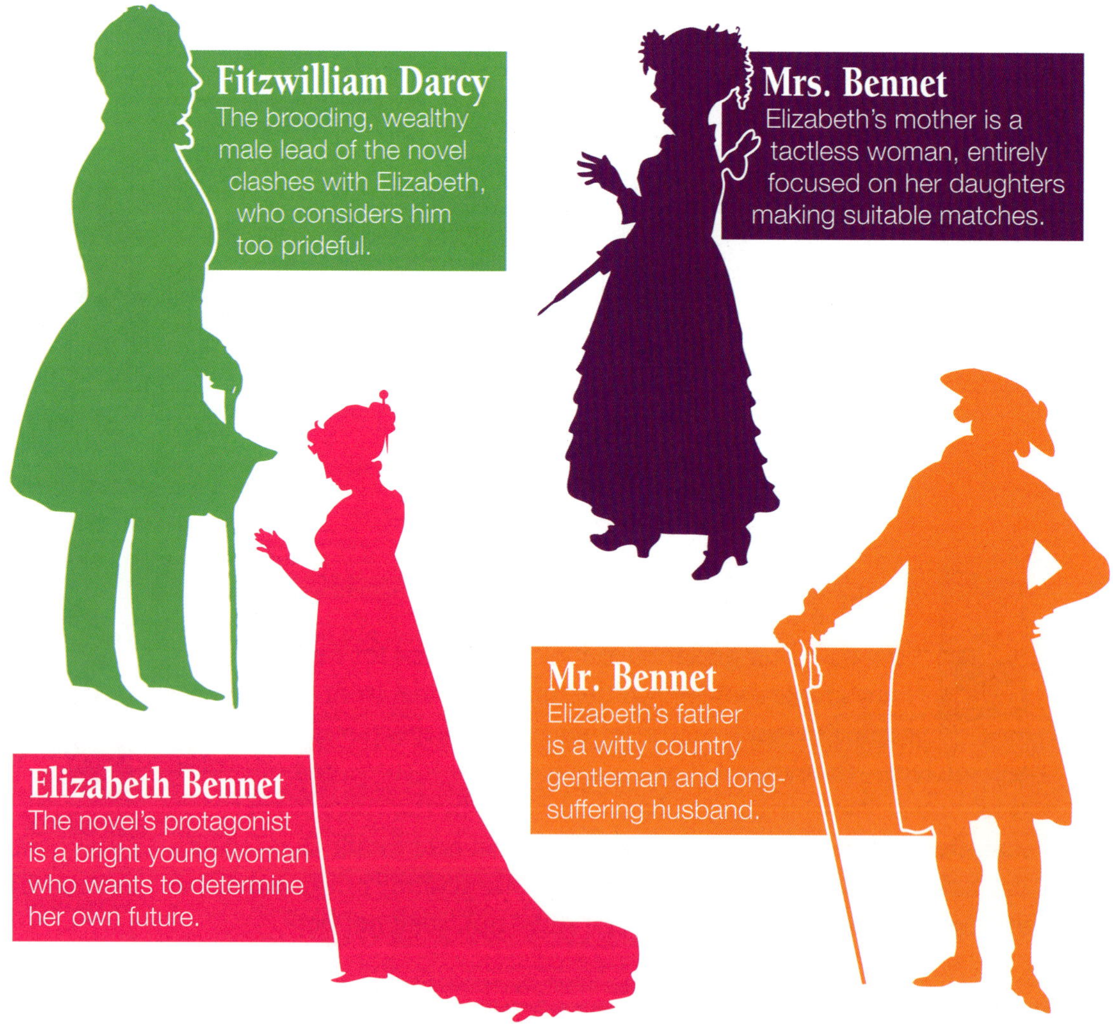

Fitzwilliam Darcy
The brooding, wealthy male lead of the novel clashes with Elizabeth, who considers him too prideful.

Mrs. Bennet
Elizabeth's mother is a tactless woman, entirely focused on her daughters making suitable matches.

Mr. Bennet
Elizabeth's father is a witty country gentleman and long-suffering husband.

Elizabeth Bennet
The novel's protagonist is a bright young woman who wants to determine her own future.

Most stories have a protagonist and an antagonist. The protagonist is the central character who must resolve a conflict over the course of the story, and often develops as a character as a result of facing this conflict. Elizabeth Bennet learns much about herself and first impressions, as she interacts with young men and watches others navigate their own romances. While her conflict is primarily with herself, tensions are also caused by societal expectations and legal limitations on women at the time, as well as people who represent these issues.

The antagonist is the character or force who stands in opposition to the protagonist. In some cases, he or she creates or represents the conflict that the protagonist has to overcome. Lady Catherine de Bourgh can be seen as an antagonist for the way she attempts to end the relationship between Elizabeth and Mr. Darcy. More importantly, she represents the societal issues working against Elizabeth and the prejudicial thinking that Elizabeth herself had to work through.

There are many characters that assist in moving the plot forward. Dynamic characters, such as Mr. Darcy, change throughout the story, usually after facing conflict. A static character, such as Mr. Collins, does not undergo changes. A flat character, such as Lydia Bennet, has only one distinguishing personality trait, while a round character, such as Mr. Bennet, has a more complex personality.

TEACHER NOTES

First Hand

Sloane St.: Monday (May 24)

Analyze the letter that Austen wrote to her sister Cassandra on May 24, 1813, and the allusions to *Pride and Prejudice's* characters it contains.

1. In your opinion, what process of character development did Austen adopt? Support your theory with passages of the text.
2. Why did Austen define her female characters through their married names? Why were their appearance and fashion primary elements of characterization?

More

Character Development in *Pride and Prejudice*

Analyze the characters in *Pride and Prejudice* using the descriptions on the character map and excerpts from each character. Then, choose a character and answer the following questions.

1. Which of the writer's techniques are most effective at revealing this character's traits? Why?
2. In what ways is the characterization of this character ineffective? What could be done to improve this character's function in the novel? Defend your ideas with evidence.

EXTENSION ACTIVITY

Creating a Literary Device Analysis Booklet

Students will analyze the author's use of a literary device in the novel, and create a booklet to present this analysis. An exemplary literary device analysis booklet will meet the following criteria.

- Defines the chosen literary device accurately and in detail
- Places the definition of the literary device at the beginning of the booklet
- Provides strong, specific examples of how this literary device is used in the novel
- Describes examples in detail, with quotations properly integrated
- Includes thorough analysis of the use, purpose, and effectiveness of each example of how the chosen literary device is used in the novel
- Arranges all pages logically
- Examples are organized chronologically
- Provides no more than one example and its analysis per page
- Creates a neat, well-organized, and attractive booklet
- Booklet is colorful and displays the student's creativity
- Uses illustrations to represent the chosen literary device and the examples of how it is used in the novel

The Art of Storytelling

Storytelling is a way to entertain, engage with others, teach, or communicate perspectives on society. A narrative, or story, is a series of events that is often logically arranged. When writing his or her story, a writer structures the narrative in a particular way. The writer can also use different types of literary devices to create a distinct style and to convey the narrative's overall message. In order to tell her story effectively, Austen structured her narrative, created a plot, and used a number of literary devices in *Pride and Prejudice*.

Structure of a Narrative

Each narrative has a structure, which writers keep in mind when creating a story. The most common narrative structure, known as dramatic structure or Freytag's Pyramid, consists of five main components, which are all used in *Pride and Prejudice*.

Freytag's Pyramid

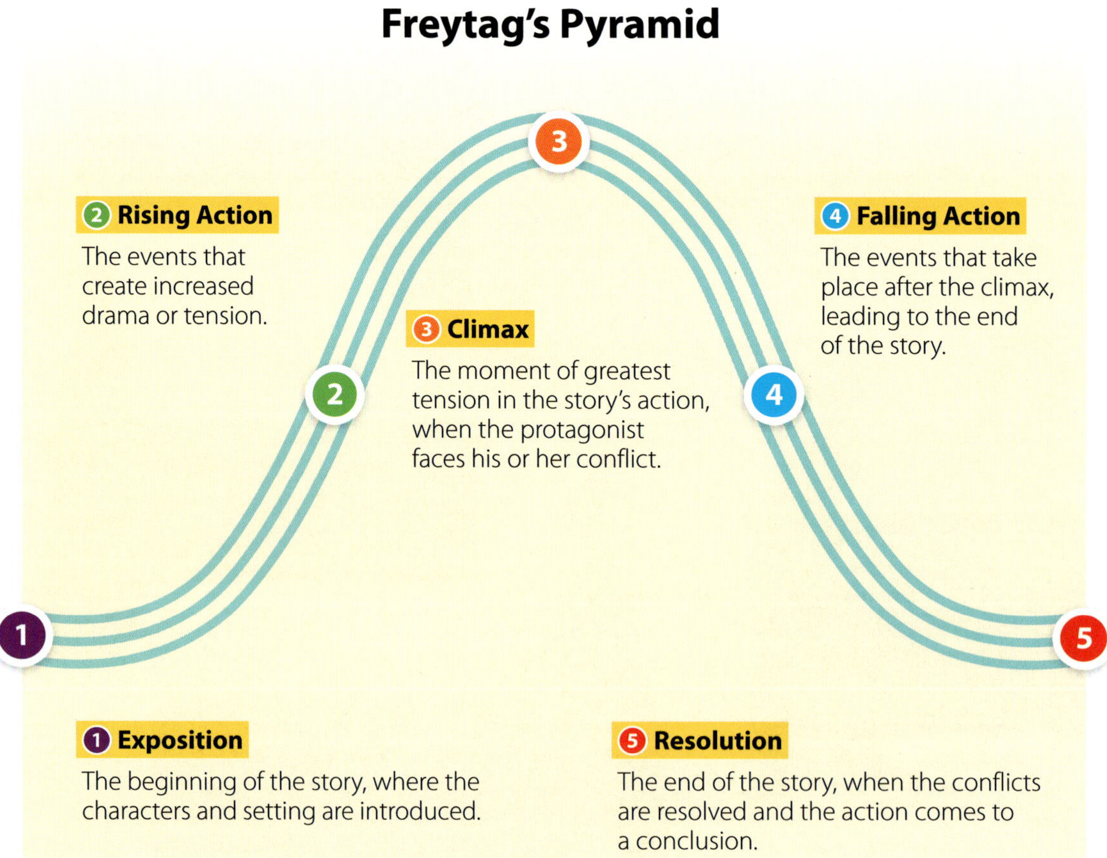

Plot

Every narrative needs to have a plot. Plot is the series of actions that propel the story forward. The plotline is the order in which events, or plot points, take place. These events build on each other and are organized in a logical manner. Each event causes the next event to happen, thus creating the narrative.

Plot Points in Chapter 3 of *Pride and Prejudice*

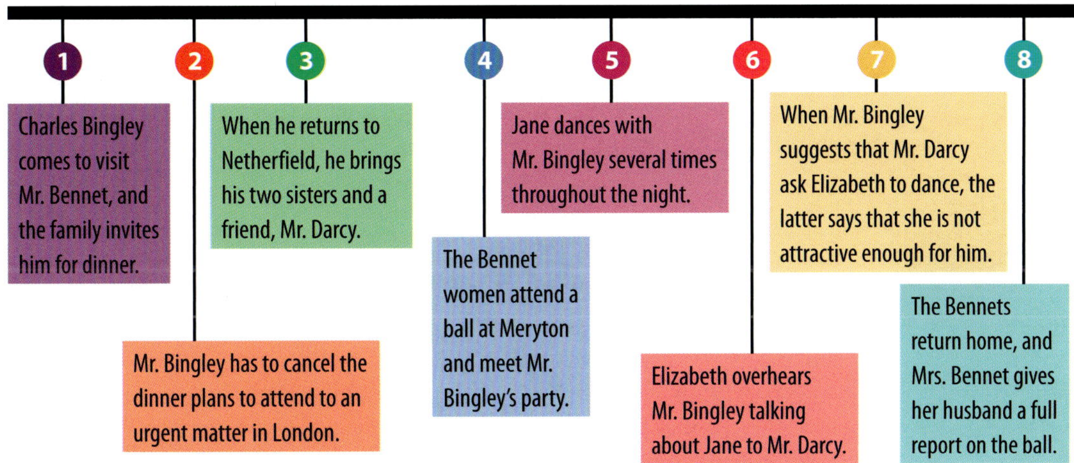

Literary Devices

A literary device is any particular feature of a work of literature that can be identified, studied, and analyzed. There are two types of literary devices. These are literary elements and literary techniques.

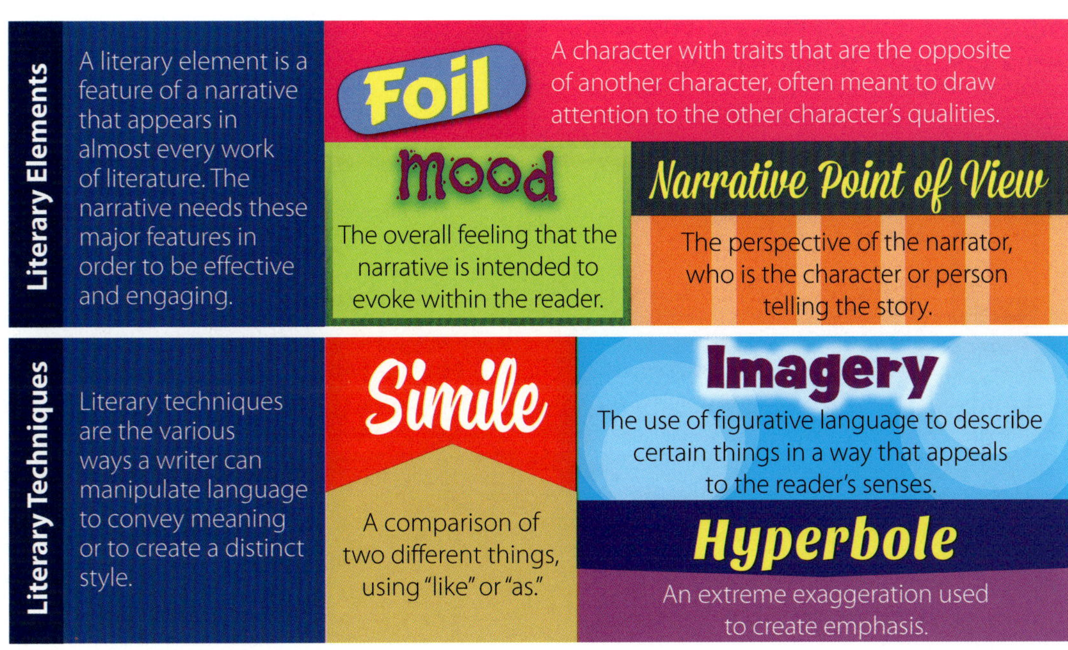

TEACHER NOTES

Weblink

The Masculine Pen: Character and Correspondence in *Pride and Prejudice*

Examine the use of letters as a literary device in *Pride and Prejudice*.

1. What is the function of letters in *Pride and Prejudice*? Why are letters used as a narrative device in the novel? What effects does this have? Give specific examples.
2. How was the use of letters as a narrative device influenced by the social conventions of the Georgian era? Why?

Examples of Literary Techniques from the Novel

Analyze the author's use of literary techniques and how they contribute to the narrative of *Pride and Prejudice*.

1. Choose one literary technique used in the novel. In what particular way did the author use this literary technique? How effective was its usage?
2. What arguments can be made for the use of your chosen literary technique in a text? If this technique were overused or underutilized, what effect might it have on an author's work?

EXTENSION ACTIVITY

Analyzing a Newspaper Article

Students will assess a newspaper article and write an analysis. An exemplary analysis will meet the following criteria.

- Identifies the topic of the article
- Identifies the main points and opinions presented in the article
- Identifies the writer of the article
- Presents information about the writer and infers how his or her life may have shaped this opinion
- Assesses the writer's reliability
- Analyzes how the writer makes his or her argument
- Uses evidence from the article to show how the writer supports his or her argument
- Analyzes the writer's use of literary devices to enhance the article
- Differentiates between the facts and opinions presented in the article
- Identifies when and where the article was published, and determines its intended audience
- Identifies and understands the goals of the article
- Assesses the effectiveness of the format (a newspaper opinion article) in presenting the writer's argument
- Connects the article to the societal and historical context in which it was written
- Infers what is not said about this topic in the article
- Identifies what information is unintentionally implied in the article
- Infers what other opinions may be presented about this topic and who may be most likely to express them
- Uses a number of other resources to analyze the context of the article

Theme in the Novel

The theme of a story is the underlying idea or position about the topic of the overall work. It is often a general, universal statement about life. Sometimes, the theme is clearly stated, and other times it is subtly suggested.

A theme is different from the topic of a literary work. While a topic is the subject of a work, a theme makes a statement about the topic in question. Theme can be expressed through the events that take place in the story, the ideas repeated along the way, and the lessons the characters learn. The theme of a story is often open to interpretation. A reader may have to examine many different aspects of a work of literature in order to form an opinion about its themes.

Values

Closely related to the novel's themes are the values held by the story's characters. In any narrative, different characters uphold different values. These values are revealed through the words and actions of the characters. In some cases, a character's values will reflect those of the story's writer. Sometimes, these values will inform or become the basis of a particular theme in the novel. Austen's opinions on society reflect her values and can be examined in relation to the themes of *Pride and Prejudice*.

Major Themes of *Pride and Prejudice*

Pride and Prejudice is an amusing narrative that also acts as a commentary on marriage, the role of women, and class structure in the first years of the nineteenth century. With wit and a clever perspective, this story illustrates how first impressions do not always tell the whole story. True to its title, the novel explores themes of pride, **prejudice**, and class.

Pride

"If his own vanity, however, did not mislead him, he was the cause, his pride and caprice were the cause, of all that Jane had suffered, and still continued to suffer. He had ruined for a while every hope of happiness for the most affectionate, generous heart in the world; and no one could say how lasting an evil he might have inflicted."

Chapter 33

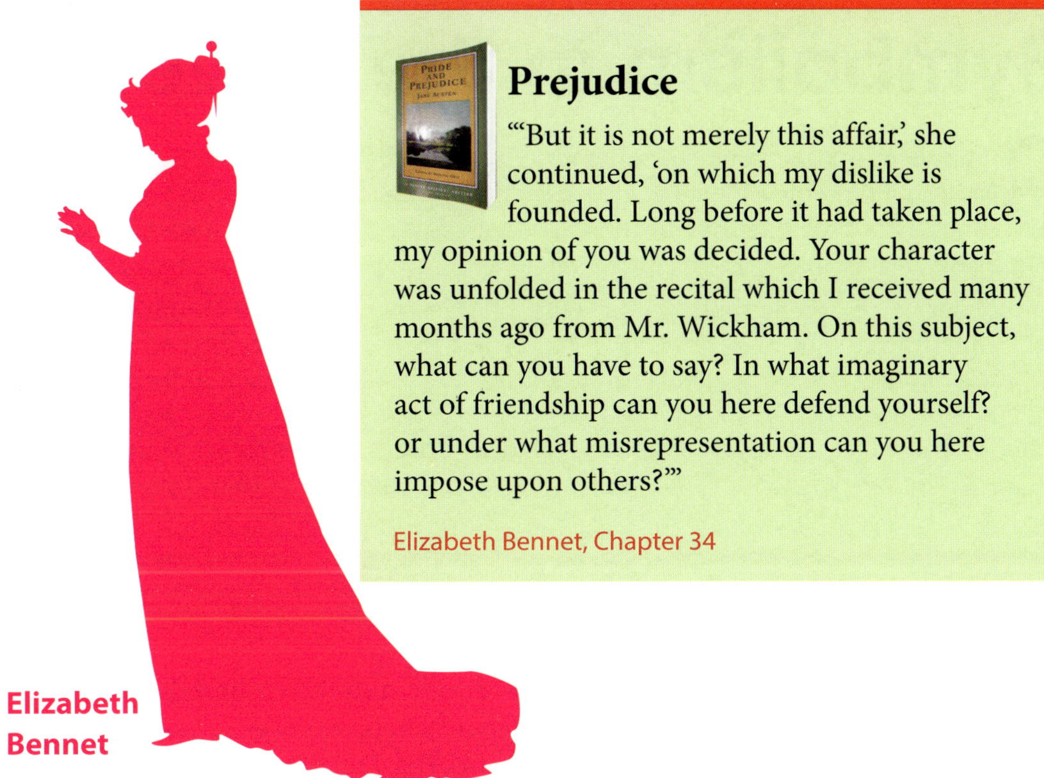

Prejudice

"'But it is not merely this affair,' she continued, 'on which my dislike is founded. Long before it had taken place, my opinion of you was decided. Your character was unfolded in the recital which I received many months ago from Mr. Wickham. On this subject, what can you have to say? In what imaginary act of friendship can you here defend yourself? or under what misrepresentation can you here impose upon others?'"

Elizabeth Bennet, Chapter 34

Class

"Her air was not conciliating, nor was her manner of receiving them such as to make her visitors forget their inferior rank. She was not rendered formidable by silence; but whatever she said was spoken in so authoritative a tone as marked her self-importance."

Chapter 29

Secondary Themes

Secondary themes are those that are not heavily emphasized in the narrative. While it does not play as large a role as a major theme, a secondary theme adds another layer to the ideas presented by the story, allowing for a more complex narrative and deeper literary analysis. Examples of secondary themes explored in *Pride and Prejudice* include family, marriage, and love.

TEACHER NOTES

Weblink

I Learned Everything I Needed to Know About Marriage From Pride and Prejudice

Analyze the article from *The Atlantic* about this secondary theme of *Pride and Prejudice*.

1. Why is one of the secondary themes of *Pride and Prejudice* more relevant to contemporary readers than the primary themes? Formulate some theories and cite examples from the text.
2. How can a literary theme be connected to the reader's real life? Choose another theme from *Pride and Prejudice* and interpret the connection in light of the example set by this article.

More

Major and Secondary Themes

Analyze the author's development of themes over the course of the novel.

1. Choose a secondary theme from this spread and analyze its appearances in the novel. How does this theme first emerge? Which is the most poignant example of this theme in the novel?
2. What particular commentary might the author be making about life as a result of this theme's presence in the text? Explain and defend your ideas.
3. Choose a major theme presented on pages 16–17. In what ways does your chosen secondary theme relate to this major theme? Does it deepen or detract from the major theme? How or in what way?

EXTENSION ACTIVITY

Creating a Symbolism Poster

Students will choose one of the other symbols listed on page 19 and analyze its role in the novel. They will then create a poster to present their analysis. An exemplary symbolism poster will meet the following criteria.

- Presents a clear purpose that is conveyed throughout the poster
- Shows an understanding of the concept of symbolism and the role it plays in the novel
- Provides an in-depth analysis of what the symbol represents
- Discusses the role the symbol plays in the novel
- Clearly indicates where the symbol appears in the novel
- Uses specific, detailed examples from the text to support the analysis
- Makes clear connections to the text
- Properly integrates all quotations
- Organizes the information in a logical, easy-to-read manner
- Includes high-quality graphics that relate to the symbol and effectively enhance understanding of the topic
- Features clear and concise writing
- Uses correct spelling, grammar, and punctuation
- Clearly labels items of importance
- Headings and subheadings are clear and easy to read
- Uses layout to creatively enhances the information
- Creates a poster that is attractive in terms of layout, design, and organization
- Shows a strong effort by the student

Symbolism in the Novel

Symbolism is a literary technique writers use to help convey theme. A symbol is often a tangible object to which a writer lends deeper meaning. Other times, action or dialogue in the narrative can be symbolic of a specific idea or theme.

Symbolism helps to give the story's events, characters, and themes a universal feel. Sometimes, it sheds light on how the writer feels about specific concepts and ideas. When studying a work of literature, the reader can gain a deeper understanding of the story by identifying and analyzing the symbols used by the writer. Some works, such as *Pride and Prejudice*, do not use extensive symbolism, but, as in the case of Austen's novel, feature one major symbol that represents a key idea.

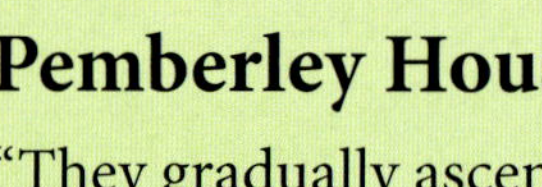

Pemberley House

"They gradually ascended for half a mile, and then found themselves at the top of a considerable eminence, where the wood ceased, and the eye was instantly caught by Pemberley House, situated on the opposite side of a valley, into which the road, with some abruptness, wound. It was a large, handsome, stone building, standing well on rising ground, and backed by a ridge of high woody hills;—and in front, a stream of some natural importance was swelled into greater, but without any artificial appearance. Its banks were neither formal, nor falsely adorned. Elizabeth was delighted. She had never seen a place for which nature had done more, or where natural beauty had been so little counteracted by an awkward taste."

Chapter 43

Pemberley as a Symbol

The main use of symbolism in *Pride and Prejudice* comes through the houses and estates owned by the characters. The best example of this is Pemberley. While the manors in the novel represent the wealth and status of their owners, they also illustrate their true nature. When Elizabeth visits Pemberley, she is impressed with its subtle elegance, which is in contrast to the opulence and extravagance found in other grand homes. This represents Mr. Darcy's true nature, distinguishing him from others with wealth and status. Another feature of Pemberley that represents Mr. Darcy's character is the stream that runs near the house. While the stream, much like Darcy, has some "natural importance" that reflects his pride, it is not artificial, which symbolizes his honest, genuine nature.

A Turning Point

"Whilst wandering on in this slow manner, they were again surprized, and Elizabeth's astonishment was quite equal to what it had been at first, by the sight of Mr. Darcy approaching them, and at no great distance … Elizabeth, however astonished, was at least more prepared for an interview than before, and resolved to appear and to speak with calmness, if he really intended to meet them. For a few moments, indeed, she felt that he would probably strike into some other path. This idea lasted while a turning in the walk concealed him from their view; the turning passed, he was immediately before them. With a glance she saw that he had lost none of his recent civility; and, to imitate his politeness, she began, as they met, to admire the beauty of the place."

Chapter 43

Pemberley is also an important setting and symbol because this is where Elizabeth and Darcy's relationship reaches a turning point. Elizabeth's heart is captured by this beautiful estate, much in the same way that Darcy begins to attract her attention. Their meeting at Pemberley represents the efforts on both their parts to move past the prejudices that led them to clash, and understand each other as they see their true selves.

Other Houses as Symbols

The Bennets' Home

The Bennets' home in Longbourn represents the family's station, in that it is a modest, but well-kept house. While it does not have the size or grandeur of the manors featured in the novel, it is a respectable home, fitting of a country gentleman such as Mr. Bennet.

Rosings

Lady Catherine de Bourgh's estate, Rosings, is the picture of aristocratic grandness, with signs of her wealth and status at all turns. However, Elizabeth notes that the furnishings of this home are not tasteful or elegant, especially when compared with those at Pemberley. The tasteless extravagance of Rosings symbolizes Lady Catherine's focus on class and status above all else, and the negativity of that attitude toward others.

TEACHER NOTES

Weblink

Where would Mr. Darcy live now? Jane Austen's 'Pemberley' is on sale

Read the article from *The Telegraph* and analyze the role of Pemberley, both in Austen's *Pride and Prejudice* and its screen adaptations.

1. Why was the English country house considered,"a great symbol of success"? How does this consideration resonate in Austen's novel? Cite evidence from the text.
2. In your opinion, why are English country houses still seen by many people today as a status symbol? Is this an outdated notion? Why or why not? Support your view with specific examples.

More

Symbolism in *Pride and Prejudice*

Analyze how a specific symbol contributes to the novel's overall structure and meaning.

1. How does the symbol of the house demonstrate Austen's purpose and perspective? Cite thorough textual evidence to support your analysis.
2. How is this symbol connected to the historical context of *Pride and Prejudice*?
3. Would the house still have been the main symbol in the novel if *Pride and Prejudice* was written in our modern world? What other symbols can you think of that might be more familiar to a contemporary reader?

EXTENSION ACTIVITY

Analyzing a Video

Students will watch and assess a video related to a component of the novel, and write an analysis of the video. An exemplary video analysis will meet the following criteria.

- Identifies the purpose of the video
- Identifies the intended audience of the video
- Describes how the content of the video is presented
- Summarizes the information and opinions presented in the video
- Analyzes the quality of the content presented in the video
- Assesses the effectiveness of the video
- Discusses the technical aspects of the video and whether or not these enhance the content
- Determines whether the images and graphics used in the video relate to the content
- Determines whether the video is easy to follow and understand
- Gives the analysis a clear and consistent purpose
- Organizes the analysis in a logical, effective manner
- Presents a strong, clear argument about the video
- Provides strong and accurate details to support the argument about the video
- Considers other perspectives on the purpose and effectiveness of the video
- Makes connections between the video and the novel
- Properly integrates quotations from the video
- Cites all sources used in the analysis

The Use of Language

The way in which a writer uses language is vital to any written work. Diction is a writer's word choice, which is used to enhance the narrative and its messages. Austen's use of language in *Pride and Prejudice*, including diction, gives her novel a distinct feel and helps to create a memorable narrative.

What Is Style?

Style is the way a specific work is written. A writer's style consists of a number of literary devices, such as diction, syntax, imagery, and point of view, used in the work. The author's choice of literary devices gives the written work a discernible feel and shapes its style. Many writers are known for their particular styles of writing. Style is used to present information to the readers and to convey the writer's purpose. The purpose may be narrative, persuasive, expository, or descriptive. There are some forms and purposes of writing, such as journalistic or academic works, that follow specific style guidelines.

What Is Voice?

A writer's voice is more specific than his or her style. While voice involves similar choices to style regarding how a work is written, voice is unique to the writer. It is the writer's individual personality and form of expression, a distinct voice giving life to his or her written work.

The Witty Voice of Austen

"It is a truth universally acknowledged, that a single man in possession of a good fortune must be in want of a wife. However little known the feelings or views of such a man may be on his first entering a neighbourhood, this truth is so well fixed in the minds of the surrounding families, that he is considered as the rightful property of some one or other of their daughters."

Chapter 1

The well-known opening lines of *Pride and Prejudice* set up the circumstances of the story and inciting incident, and also introduce the reader to a sharp, witty narrator. Austen's voice is one of the features that makes the novel so engaging. Her commentary on society through this narrative is filled with humor and honesty. Her distinct style creates a light, sparkling tone to the story.

Elizabeth and Mr. Darcy

"'I remember hearing you once say, Mr. Darcy, that you hardly every forgave, that your resentment once created was unappeasable. You are very cautious, I suppose, as to its being created?'
'I am,' said he, with a firm voice.
'And never allow yourself to be blinded by prejudice?'
'I hope not.'
'It is particularly incumbent on those who never change their opinion, to be secure of judging properly at first.'
'May I ask to what these questions tend?'
'Merely to the illustration of your character,' said she, endeavouring to shake off her gravity. 'I am trying to make it out.'"

Elizabeth Bennet and Fitzwilliam Darcy, Chapter 18

The Use of Dialogue in *Pride and Prejudice*

The novel relies heavily on dialogue, and it is through snappy, clever lines that Elizabeth and Mr. Darcy first clash, and eventually come together. They are both quick-witted and intelligent, traits that Austen reveals through their dialogue. These abilities distinguish them from the other characters, and illustrate that they are intellectual equals. Austen also uses dialogue to provide humor, particularly through Mr. and Mrs. Bennet. Mr. Bennet proves himself a sarcastic and witty character, much like Elizabeth, while Mrs. Bennet's near-hysteria and narrow-mindedness are illustrated through her dialogue. Together, the conversations between the Bennets result in some of the novel's most humorous moments.

Mr. and Mrs. Bennet

"'Mr. Bennet, how can you abuse your own children in such a way? You take delight in vexing me. You have no compassion on my poor nerves.'
'You mistake me, my dear. I have a high respect for your nerves. They are my old friends. I have heard you mention them with consideration these twenty years at least.'
'Ah! you do not know what I suffer.'
'But I hope you will get over it, and live to see many young men of four thousand a year come into the neighbourhood.'"

Mr. and Mrs. Bennet, Chapter 1

TEACHER NOTES

Video

***Pride and Prejudice* (1940) – Archery**

Compare and contrast the dialogue of *Pride and Prejudice*, considering this clip from the 1940 film adaptation and the clip from the 1995 television adaptation on page 11.

1. How does the tone of the 1940 film dialogue correspond to the tone used in Austen's novel? In what ways are they similar? How are they different?
2. Compare and contrast the dialogue of the 1940 and 1995 screen adaptations of *Pride and Prejudice*. Are they faithful to the original dialogue of the novel? Which screen adaptation reproduces the novel's dialogue more effectively? In your opinion, how does the time of production of these adaptations influence their adherence to the novel? What are the effects of this?

Weblink

***Pride and Prejudice* and the art of conversation**

Assess the importance of dialogue in *Pride and Prejudice*.

1. In *Pride and Prejudice,* how is the book's narrator,"having a conversation with us: the readers"? Explain your answer using the excerpts from the text.
2. How does the dialogue between the characters differ from the dialogue between the narrator and the reader? Describe Austen's different uses of these two types of dialogue.

EXTENSION ACTIVITY

Writing a Book Review

Students will write a book review of the novel. An exemplary book review will meet the following criteria.

- Grabs the reader's attention with a creative headline
- Begins with an engaging lead to pull the reader into the article
- Introduces the title of the novel, the author, and the genre
- Provides a brief plot description that does not give away the entire story, and makes the reader want to learn more about the novel
- Supports arguments about the novel with accurate and detailed information
- Organizes the review and its arguments in a concise, clear, and logical manner
- Fits the format and style of a book review
- Follows the conventions of print or online journalism
- Demonstrates creativity in their approach
- Writes with a unique, engaging voice and perspective
- Provides fresh insight into the novel
- Provides an honest, authentic opinion on the novel
- Gives a clear recommendation on the novel, backed up by specific textual evidence
- Uses correct spelling, grammar, and punctuation

Impact of the Novel at the Time of Publishing

When Austen published *Pride and Prejudice* in 1813, there were not many female novelists in the English-speaking world. Her novel came at a time when many female writers used a particular topic and tone in their writings, and at the time when the novel was developing into its modern form. Austen's well-received book was one of the stories that would lead her to becoming a writer whose novels were very much enjoyed at this time.

Critical and Reader Responses

As Austen published *Pride and Prejudice* anonymously, no one but her family knew of her writing career during her life. *Pride and Prejudice* and her other novels received critical acclaim and praise from readers at publication, and brought Austen some financial success. Critics complimented her entertaining narratives and honest portrayals of everyday situations.

A Royal Reader

The Prince Regent bought a set of Austen's novels for each royal residence and commanded she dedicate *Emma* to him. Although Austen was not fond of the Prince Regent, likely due to his excessive and self-indulgent tendencies, she could not disobey a royal command. Her dedication was respectful, yet hinted at her feelings. It reads, "To His Royal Highness the Prince Regent, this work is, by His Royal Highness's permission, most respectfully dedicated to His Royal Highness by His dutiful and obedient humble servant, the Author."

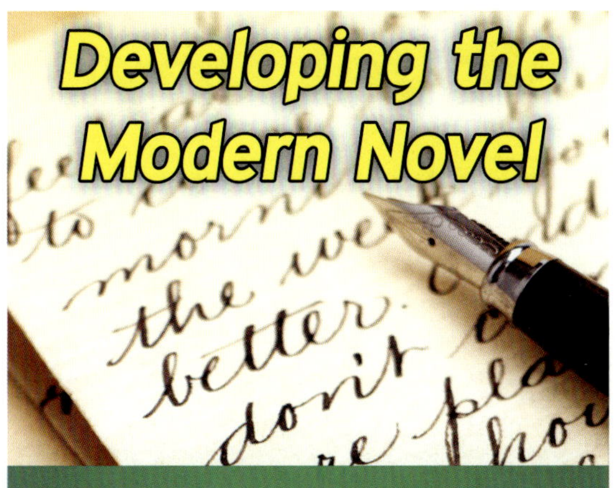

Austen lived at a time when reading novels was a popular pastime, but many novels tended toward sensational tales that were not always well written. In commenting on this kind of literature in a letter to a friend, she wrote, "I must keep to my own style and go on in my own Way; And though I may never succeed again in that, I am convinced that I should totally fail in any other." Austen's novels take a completely different approach from what was in style at the time, by portraying everyday people, places, and relationships, which were relatable to readers. Her approach led to the development of the modern novel.

Female Writers and Domestic Fiction

During her career, Austen was seen as a "domestic" novelist. In the late eighteenth and early nineteenth centuries, domestic fiction was connected to female writers and portrayed the domestic sphere of women, which was the ruling ideology of the time. However, Austen used this format to make intelligent, thoughtful commentary on society, and created a style that she is now known for, proving that domestic fiction could convey meaningful messages.

London publisher, **Thomas Egerton** bought *Pride and Prejudice* in **1812 for £110**.

The **first print run** of the novel in **January 1813** printed about **1,500 copies.**

In 2012, a **first edition** of *Pride and Prejudice* sold for **$68,500**.

TEACHER NOTES

First Hand

Review of *Pride and Prejudice* from *The Critical Review*

Analyze the 1813 review of *Pride and Prejudice.*

1. What is the tone of the review? Why does the author describe the novel as, "a story of a whole family"? Do you agree with this assertion? Defend your opinion with solid arguments.
2. Is the "realistic nature of the scenes" an aspect that the contemporary reader can still recognize today? Why or why not?

Weblink

"Your Kind Recommendation": the Prince Regent's Copy of *Emma*

Explore the events linked to the royal invitation to Austen and her dedication of *Emma* to the Prince Regent.

1. What do these events tell us about the public reception of Austen's works? Justify your answer.
2. Why did Austen disapprove of the conduct of the Prince Regent? How is her disapproval of such types of conduct evident in the voices of the characters in *Pride and Prejudice*, or in her other books? List specific examples.

Impact of the Novel Now

Two hundred years after its publication, *Pride and Prejudice* is widely regarded as a literary classic. Austen is now considered to be one of English literature's best writers, and her novel is studied academically and enjoyed by readers all over the world. Elizabeth Bennet is one of English literature's best-loved heroines, and the novel that is arguably Austen's best-known work continues to resonate with modern readers today.

About **60,000** people visit the **Jane Austen Centre** in Bath, Somerset, United Kingdom, **each year.**

It was estimated in 2013 that **up to 50,000 copies** of *Pride and Prejudice* are sold in the United Kingdom alone **every year.**

In 2002, **The Guardian** listed *Pride and Prejudice* as one of the **top 100** books of all time.

Enduring Legacy

Austen's legacy and the popularity of her novels, especially *Pride and Prejudice*, continue today because of the relatability of her stories. The challenges faced by her protagonists, while navigating the world and learning about themselves, are just as relatable and meaningful as they were when her novels were first published. In 2013, readers across the globe celebrated the 200th anniversary of *Pride and Prejudice*'s publication. The Jane Austen Centre in Bath, the city where Austen lived for five years, hosted a 12-hour online broadcast of the novel read aloud as part of the festivities. The Centre also hosts an annual Jane Austen Festival, which some visitors attend in Regency-era costumes.

Film Adaptations

An early film adaptation of *Pride and Prejudice* in 1940 cast Laurence Olivier in the role of Mr. Darcy. The 2005 film, starring Keira Knightly and Matthew Macfadyen, was well-received by critics for its visuals and the lead actors' performances. Arguably the best-known adaptation of the novel is the critically acclaimed 1995 miniseries, starring Jennifer Ehle and Colin Firth.

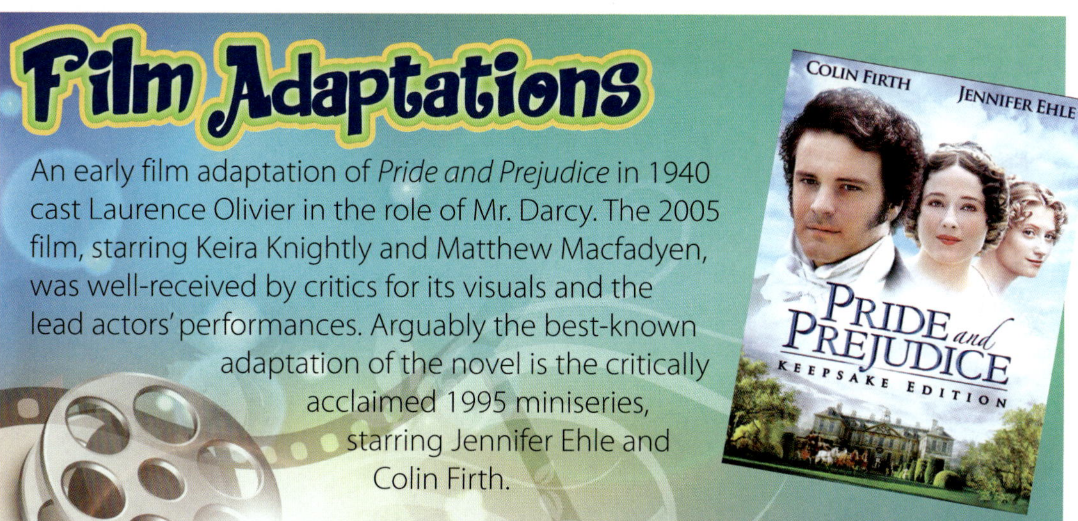

Musical Adaptations

Pride and Prejudice has been adapted for the stage several times, including a number of musical adaptations. *First Impressions*, a musical comedy based on a dramatization of the novel, opened on Broadway in 1959. In 2008, a new adaptation, *Austen's Pride and Prejudice, A New Musical*, was performed in Rochester, New York, as a concert. This version starred Broadway performers Laura Osnes and Colin Donnell as Elizabeth and Mr. Darcy, respectively. The musical then played at the New York Musical Theatre Festival, and in 2015, had its world premier at New York's La Mirada Theatre.

Inventive Adaptations

In recent years, there have been a number of adaptations of *Pride and Prejudice* that put a different spin on the story. *The Lizzie Bennet Diaries* is a web series comprised of video blog-style episodes featuring a modern-day grad student named Lizzie. The television miniseries *Lost in Austen* follows a contemporary fan of the novel who suddenly finds herself inside the story, while the book and film *Pride and Prejudice and Zombies* adds a supernatural element to Austen's classic story.

TEACHER NOTES

Video

***My Name is Lizzie Bennet* - Ep: 1**
The Lizzie Bennet Diaries

Compare the first episode of the web series, *The Lizzie Bennet Diaries*, with the first chapter of *Pride and Prejudice.*

1. How has the opening of *Pride and Prejudice* been adapted to fit a web series? Do the main features of Austen's characters correspond to the characters presented in the web series? Support your answers with examples.
2. How do you explain the success of the web series? In your opinion, is the web series accessible to non-readers of Austen? Why or why not?

Weblink

Back to Pemberley: 8 *Pride and Prejudice* Adaptations

Explore the different screen adaptations of *Pride and Prejudice* described in this blog entry.

1. What is the tone of the blog entry? What aspects does the blog writer emphasize in her post? In your opinion, why are these aspects often discussed in relation to Austen's novels and their adaptations? Argue your view.
2. What makes *Pride and Prejudice* so easily adaptable to different cultural and chronological contexts? Justify your answer.

EXTENSION ACTIVITY

Creating a Timeline

Students will explore a topic related to the novel and create a timeline to present their research on historical events connected to this topic. An exemplary timeline will meet the following criteria.

- Includes the most significant events pertaining to the topic to be compared and analyzed
- Includes interesting events
- Uses accurate information for all events, including date, location, and major details
- Orders the events in a chronological sequence
- Describes each event with accurate, vivid, and specific details
- Presents the topic from three or more perspectives
- Inspires the reader to ask thoughtful questions regarding the events and perspectives presented in the timeline
- Uses correct spelling, grammar, and punctuation
- Presents the timeline in a visually attractive and striking manner
- Presents the timeline in a neat, organized manner that is logical and easy to follow
- Uses creativity to present the timeline in an engaging manner
- Effectively communicates the historical information relating to the topic
- Supports each event with reliable sources
- Expresses a clear purpose for creating the timeline
- Enhances the reader's understanding of the topic
- Includes a correctly formatted bibliography of all sources used to create the timeline

Perspectives on Marriage and Inheritance

One of the major societal issues at the heart of *Pride and Prejudice* is that of the legal rights afforded to women regarding money and property. While Mrs. Bennet's overbearing and hysterical focus on marrying off her daughters provides humor in the novel, her concern was valid for mothers of young women in the early nineteenth century. Certain laws prohibited most women from inheriting land and capital from their fathers at this time, making them dependent on their husbands for financial security.

Marriage and Female Inheritance Law Timeline

1700s

1771 New York passes a law that requires a man to obtain his wife's permission before selling property that she brought into the marriage.

1791 The French Revolution ushers in equal inheritance rights for women, which are later taken away.

1800s

1839 Mississippi becomes the first state to give women the right to own property in their own names.

1848 New York becomes the first state to pass the Married Women's Property Act, which is later passed in all states.

1850 Iceland becomes the first country to legislate equal inheritance rights for all citizens.

As well, women were limited by marriage in what they owned. A couple's property often legally belonged to the husband, and for centuries, a woman was legally considered the property of her husband. Laws regarding inheritance, property ownership, and fair wages for women have changed dramatically since Austen's time, but this is not the case in some parts of the world.

1800s | **1900s** | **Today**

1862 American women are able to apply for land claims on their own through the Homestead Act.

1862 California's new state banking system legislates that a woman is guaranteed the right to control the money she deposits in her own bank account.

1870 The Married Women's Property Act is passed in the United Kingdom, allowing married women to maintain ownership of their property.

1881 Women in France are legally allowed to open their own bank accounts. Five years later, married women are given the right to open an account without their husbands' consent.

1922 In the United Kingdom, the Law of Property Act guarantees equal inheritance of property between a husband and wife.

1963 The Equal Pay Act is signed into law. It mandates that men and women receive equal pay for equal work, in an attempt to end gender inequality.

Today Although women have made advances in the workplace, there is still a gender pay gap, with women earning only about 80 percent of what men do for the same work. At the current rate of change, women may not reach pay equity with men until at least 2059, unless companies, individuals, and policy makers all work to close the gap.

TEACHER NOTES

Transparency–Timeline

Marriage and Female Inheritance Law Timeline

Examine the historical and cultural contexts shown on the timeline. Then, contrast and correlate its elements with the themes and events presented in *Pride and Prejudice*.

1. In what ways can historical events, culture, and social mores influence a population's perspective on women's rights? How might these elements have shaped the way a reader in the 1810s interpreted the novel?
2. How might the era in which Jane Austen wrote *Pride and Prejudice* have influenced the novel's themes and settings? Where in the novel is this most evident? Explain your reasoning.
3. Which current events, changes in laws, new ideas, or political discussions are shaping the future of womens rights? Which ideas and attitudes are still prevailing? Why?
4. How might current events and present perspectives affect the way a reader interprets the novel? Why is it important for readers to understand the era and context in which a novel is written?

EXTENSION ACTIVITY

Writing a Comparative Essay

Students will compare two literary devices used in the novel, and then write a comparative essay based on their analysis. An exemplary comparative essay will meet the following criteria.

- Consists of a one-paragraph introduction, three body paragraphs, and a one-paragraph conclusion
- Introduction includes an engaging lead statement about the topic of the essay, more detailed information about the novel, and a one-sentence thesis that specifically states the essay's argument
- Body paragraphs include a topic sentence that refers to the thesis and how the idea appears in the novel, a supporting sentence that points to this part of the novel, textual evidence of this idea from the novel, and analysis of this evidence
- Body paragraphs end with a transition to the next paragraph
- Conclusion refers to the topic of the essay and the three points presented in the body paragraphs, and restates the thesis
- Provides a thorough analysis of the literary devices in question
- Cites strong and thorough textual evidence to support analysis of what the novel says explicitly
- Presents a clear, specific thesis that indicates a high level of critical engagement
- Organizes ideas in a logical manner
- Communicates arguments in a clear, effective manner
- Properly integrates all quotations
- Correctly cites all sources used
- Correctly formats bibliography

Writing a Comparative Essay

Pride and Prejudice is brought to life with entertaining characters, beautiful settings, and themes that are relatable to modern readers. After studying the novel, write a comparative essay to explore how two literary devices are used in *Pride and Prejudice*. This could be a comparison of characters, themes, symbols, or settings. To write a comparative essay, you will need to formulate an argument. Your argument should clearly state how you feel your compared elements are similar or different. Support your argument with sufficient evidence from the novel and valid reasoning.

How to Analyze and Compare Characters

Use the chart to guide your comparison of two characters in *Pride and Prejudice*.

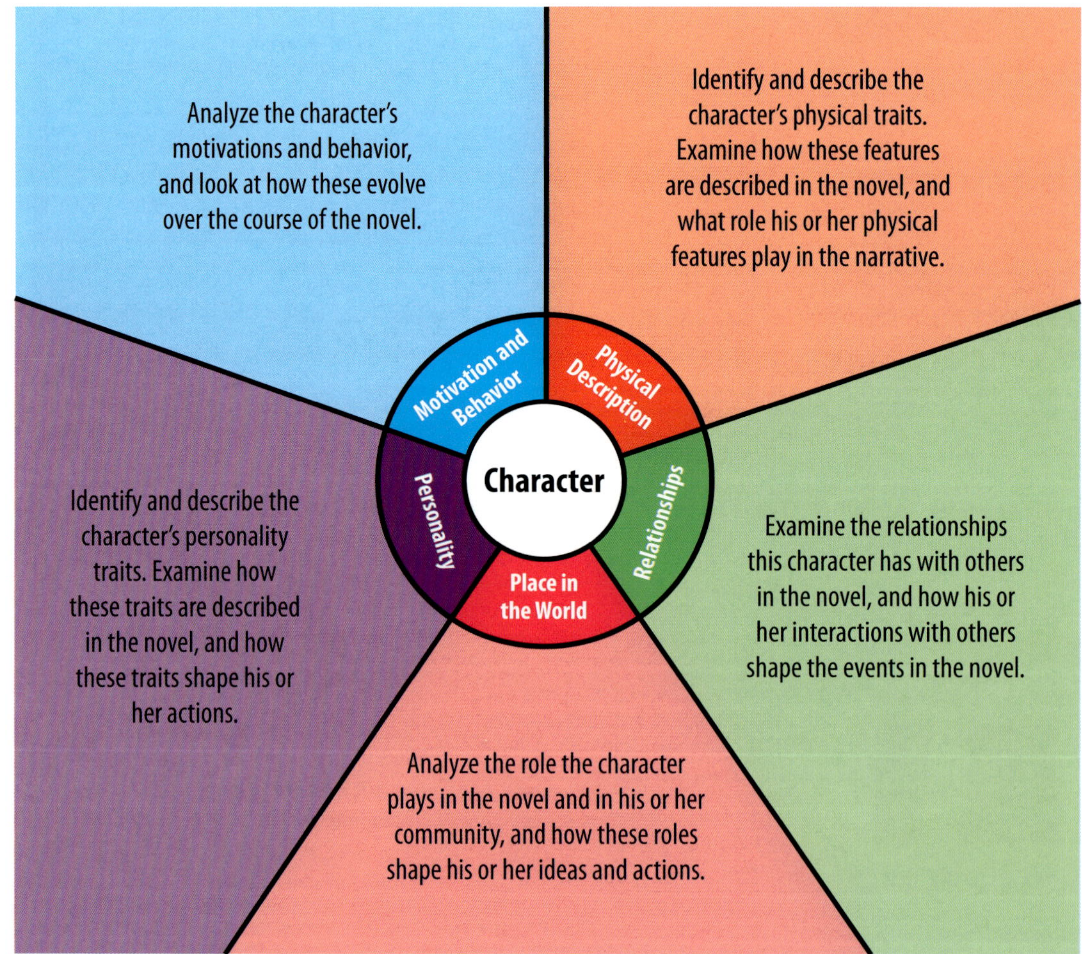

Comparing Fitzwilliam Darcy and George Wickham

Mr. Darcy

Place in the World
- Wealthy
- A member of the upper class
- Owns Pemberley
- A gentleman

Motivation and Behavior
- Class-conscious
- Awkward in expressing himself
- Becomes more aware of the feelings of others
- Changes his outlook after he is refused by Elizabeth
- Works to help Elizabeth's family

Personality
- Proud
- Intelligent
- Honest
- Aloof
- Brooding
- Honorable
- Comes off as arrogant and vain early in the novel

Physical Description
- Tall
- Fine figure
- Extremely handsome

Relationships
- Older brother of Georgiana Darcy
- Friends with Charles Bingley
- Former friend of George Wickham
- Nephew of Lady Catherine de Bourgh
- In love with Elizabeth Bennet

Mr. Wickham

Place in the World
- Officer in the local militia
- Has a disreputable past

Physical Description
- Handsome
- Fine
- Looks like the ideal officer

Motivation and Behavior
- Plays upon others' prejudices
- Works to spread lies about Mr. Darcy
- Concerned with paying off his gambling debts
- An **opportunist**

Relationships
- Former friend of Fitzwilliam Darcy
- Charms Elizabeth Bennet
- Runs away with Lydia Bennet

Personality
- Charming
- Charismatic
- Agreeable
- Dishonest
- Well-spoken

TEACHER NOTES

Transparency–Chart

Questions for Character Analysis

Analyze how specific character features, such as conflicts, motivations, relationships, place in the world, and personality affect the plot of *Pride and Prejudice*. Cite strong and thorough textual evidence to support your analysis of what the novel says explicitly as well as the inferences you may have drawn from the novel's setting, themes, and symbols.

Quiz Answers

1. B
2. D
3. D
4. A
5. B
6. C
7. A
8. D
9. B
10. B

Key Words

civility: acting in a formal, polite, and courteous manner

classes: divisions in society based on economic, cultural, or political features; these divisions determine an individual's or group's social rank

gentry: people belonging to the social class below the aristocracy; specifically dealing with the British class system

inheritance: property or capital passed to an heir on the death of the former owner

militia: a civilian military unit organized to support a regular army

moral: dealing with principles of what is right and wrong

opportunist: a person who seeks ways to gain advantages from situations, often at the expense of ethics or morals

perspectives: certain points of view or positions regarding a subject

prejudice: a preconceived opinion or idea, formed without reason or sufficient knowledge

prided: felt satisfaction related to one's skills, reputation, or possessions

society: an organized community of people interacting with each other

typhus: an infectious disease transmitted by lice and fleas

valued: held certain standards of behavior or other aspects of life as important

Literary Terms

antagonist: the character who stands in opposition to the protagonist; in some cases, the antagonist creates or represents the conflict that the protagonist faces

climax: the moment of greatest tension in the story's action

conflict: a struggle between two or more opposing forces, creating a tension that must be resolved

exposition: the beginning of the story, where the characters and setting are introduced

falling action: the events that take place after the climax, leading up to the end of the story

foil: a character with traits that are the opposite of another character, often meant to draw attention to the other character's qualities

hyperbole: an extreme exaggeration used to create emphasis

imagery: the use of figurative language to describe certain things in a way that appeals to the reader's senses

mood: the overall feeling that the narrative is intended to evoke within the reader

narrative: a logically arranged series of events presented for an audience; a story

plot: the specific action that propels a story forward

protagonist: the central character in a piece of fiction who must deal with a conflict and often undergoes some type of change as a result

resolution: the end of the story, when the problems are resolved and the action comes to a conclusion

rising action: the events that create increased drama or tension

simile: a comparison of two different things using "like" or "as"

style: the unique way that writers use language to tell their story; this can include word choice, the use of imagery, and the length and organization of sentences

symbolism: a stylistic device using symbols to represent and intensify concepts and ideas

theme: the underlying idea or position in a work that is often a general, universal statement about life

voice: a writer's distinct personality and form of expression, as shown through his or her written work

Index

LIGHTBOX

SUPPLEMENTARY RESOURCES

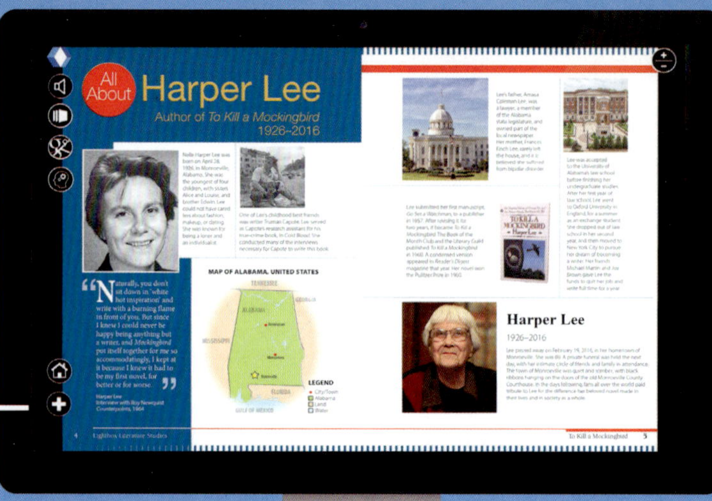

Click on the plus icon found in the bottom left corner of each spread to open additional teacher resources.

- Download and print the book's quizzes and activities
- Access curriculum correlations
- Explore additional web applications that enhance the Lightbox experience

LIGHTBOX DIGITAL TITLES

Packed full of integrated media

VIDEOS

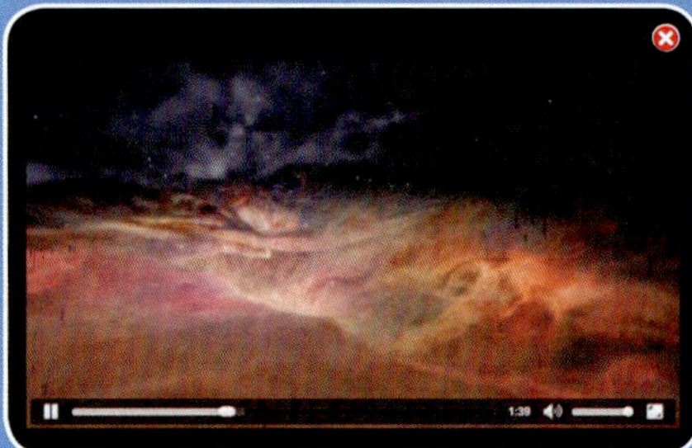

INTERACTIVE MAPS

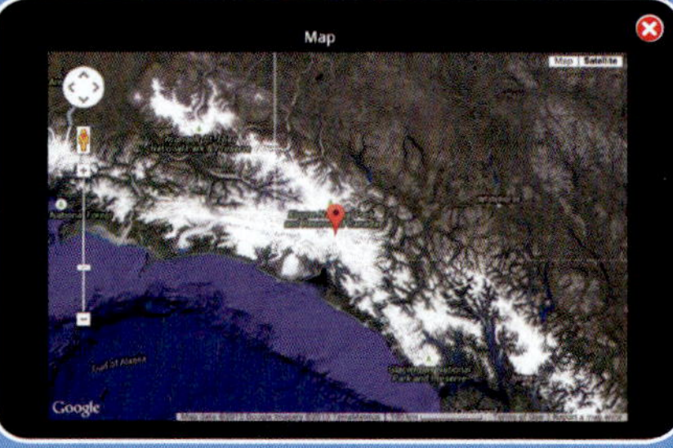

WEBLINKS

SLIDESHOWS

QUIZZES

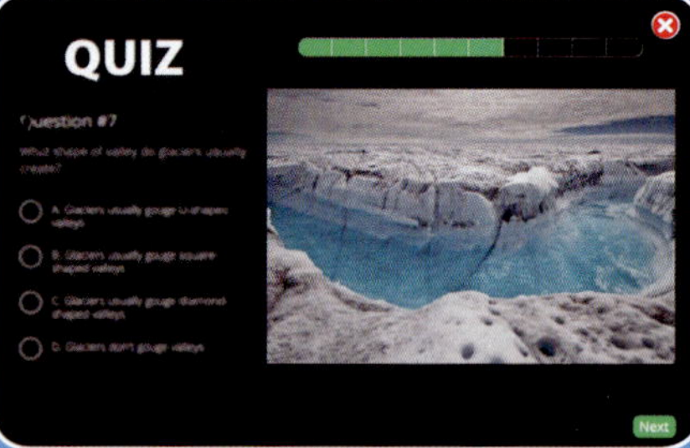

OPTIMIZED FOR

- ✓ TABLETS
- ✓ WHITEBOARDS
- ✓ COMPUTERS
- ✓ AND MUCH MORE!

Published by Smartbook Media Inc.
350 5th Avenue, 59th Floor New York, NY 10118
Website: www.openlightbox.com

Library of Congress Cataloging-in-Publication Data

Names: Whelan, Piper author.
Title: Pride and prejudice / Piper Whelan.
Description: New York : Smartbook Media Inc., [2018] | Series: Lightbox literature studies | Includes index.

Identifiers: LCCN 2016051611 (print) | LCCN 2017006303 (ebook) | ISBN 9781510520059 (hard cover : alk. paper) | ISBN 9781510520066 (multi-user ebk.)
Subjects: LCSH: Austen, Jane, 1775-1817. Pride and prejudice--Examinations--Study guides.
Classification: LCC PR4034.P72 W44 2018 (print) | LCC PR4034.P72 (ebook) | DDC 823/.7--dc23
LC record available at https://lccn.loc.gov/2016051611

Printed in Brainerd, Minnesota, United States
1 2 3 4 5 6 7 8 9 0 21 20 19 18 17

062017
042017

Editor: Katie Gillespie
Art Director: Terry Paulhus

Every reasonable effort has been made to trace ownership and to obtain permission to reprint copyright material. The publisher would be pleased to have any errors or omissions brought to its attention so that they may be corrected in subsequent printings.

The publisher acknowledges Getty Images, Alamy, iStock, and Shutterstock as its primary image suppliers for this title